BULLYPROOF
Unleash the Hero Inside Your Kid

BULLYPROOF
Unleash the Hero Inside Your Kid
VOLUME 4

CONTRIBUTING AUTHORS:
JIM HAMMONS
TRACY HAMMONS
MARK JOHNSON
CARLOS MARTIN
LYNDA NELSON
JOHN NOTTINGHAM
JASON WADLEY
RUSSELL WRIGHT

EDITORS:
MICHAEL CUDDYER
ALEX CHANGHO

BULLYPROOF
Unleash the Hero Inside Your Kid
Volume 4

Copyright © 2016 Alex Changho

All Rights Reserved. No part of this publication may be reproduced in any form or by any means, including scanning, photocopying, or otherwise without prior written permission of the copyright holder.

DEDICATION

There are a number of people who have made a difference in my life, helping me work on myself to lead others. They've worked to help hundreds or thousands of other people as well.

I'd like to recognize two in particular.

Senior Master Michael Wegmann, you have been my instructor for almost a quarter of a century. You taught me from the 5th grade to continually work on myself to be a better martial artist, better instructor, and better businessman. Thank you.

Steve Linder, you have taught me and thousands of other people how to look on the inside and master my own psychology. Thanks to you I've been able to help my own clients and others. Thank you.

TABLE OF CONTENTS

Introduction: Things Don't Always Get Better On Their Own - Alex Changho 1

Chapter 1: Bullyproof Strategies in School - Jim & Tracy Hammons 5

Chapter 2: How To A.V.O.I.D. Bullying - Jason Wadley 17

Chapter 3: You Can't Just Ignore It - Lynda Nelson 29

Chapter 4: Parents' Roles in Preventing Bullying – Carlos Martin 39

Chapter 5: Why Bullies Bully - Mark Johnson 49

Chapter 6: Confidence vs. Cockiness - Russell Wright 69

Chapter 7: Why Most "Anti-Bully" Programs Don't Work – John Nottingham 75

Chapter 8: Cyber-Bullying – The Next Generation of Bullying Brett Lechtenberg 95

The Butterfly Effect 109

Getting Involved With The Bullyproof Project 113

INTRODUCTION: THINGS DON'T ALWAYS GET BETTER ON THEIR OWN

BY ALEX CHANGHO
CARY, NORTH CAROLINA

"Let it be."

We all have hear that line. You know, from the Beatles' hit song.

"There will be an answer, let it be."

And for many situations, it works. Trying to find your path in life, deciding on what kind of car to drive… these kind of decisions can be made with time and without much effort.

Bullying is not one of these things.

It is appalling to me that there can be so much procrastination about this topic, particularly in legislation. In fact, a few weeks before the publication of the print version of this book, my home state of North Carolina overturned a law which protected kids from being bullied online, by outlawing certain forms of cyber bullying. It was found to be in violation of the 1st Amendment (the right to freedom of speech), and written as "too vague."

It's unfortunate because this law was protecting many people from bullying. Online and cyber-bullying is becoming such a major problem in our society today. In fact, in many cases, it is the predominant form of bullying that is happening.

So we have a choice. We can choose to wait for legislature to make changes (which, at least in North Carolina, they had). But of course, we are beholden to the courts and lawmakers to see if they are upheld or overturned. We can expect others to do everything for us.

Or, we can take a stand now and take the matter into our own hands.

In this volume of BULLYPROOF, we again bring together professionals who have worked with kids and teens for decades. They bring a message of personal empowerment, something that each one of us can do for ourselves and for the children and people whom we serve.

Also included in this volume are two reprinted chapters from BULLYPROOF Volume 1. Brett Lechtenberg's chapter on Cyber-Bullying is timely and ever important. And John Nottingham brings an almost contrarian point of view to what many schools promote within their hallways.

These two chapters round out the expertise of the authors who contribute to this project, with the common mission of Unleashing the Heroes Inside Our Kids!

Alex Changho is a lifestyle and business coach. With almost two decades of experience leading and motivating others, and running a business, he helps business owners integrate their life's mission and career with their personal side of their life.

An accomplished speaker and presenter, Alex is a Master NLP Practitioner and Trainer, Senior Leader with Anthony Robbins, and Master Strengths Coach.

Alex lives in North Carolina with his cat Bert.

For more information, visit www.alexchangho.com.

CHAPTER 1: BULLYPROOF STRATEGIES IN SCHOOL

BY JIM & TRACY HAMMONS
BROKEN ARROW, OKLAHOMA

As martial arts school owners in Broken Arrow, Oklahoma, we have witnessed firsthand the terrible and lasting effects that bullying can have on children. Although there are many challenges to face when trying to bullyproof kids, the reward of seeing children able to protect themselves is amazing. Between the two of us, we have over fifty years of training in martial arts and have made it our goal to bullyproof our entire town. It is such an important mission to equip children with the knowledge and skills to help them avoid bullying in their everyday lives.

Jim's Story

What's fortunate is that between the two of us, only Jim had to deal with being bullied when he was a kid. What's unfortunate is that those experiences were terrible and left their marks. When Jim was younger, he was very sickly with asthma and allergies, and didn't leave the house very much until he was about 11-years-old. At that time, back in the 70's, desegregation was still relatively new. Once Jim was healthy enough to go to school, he was sent to a predominantly black school. Because he was the kid in the bubble who had never made friends, he was instantly targeted and picked on. He was bullied and beat up by both boys and girls, and this constant and unrelenting torture is what led him to martial arts. Jim's personal experiences with bullying make him even more passionate to help ensure that no other children are subjected to the same types of torment that he experienced as a child.

What is Bullying?

It is easy for anyone to say that they are against bullying, but it helps to know what exactly is meant when the term "bullying" is used. Many people have varying definitions of what bullying is and oftentimes they will lump several behaviors together and call it bullying. When there is no clear definition, a lot can get lost in translation. To us, bullying goes beyond simply being rude or mean. If someone says something unkind about your appearance, and it happens every now and again, that gets classified as a person being rude or mean. They may or may not know that their behavior is wrong, but it cannot really be considered bullying. Even one person putting their hands on another or attacking them isn't bullying if it only happens once. Is it wrong? Of course. But is it bullying? No, not when it is an isolated incident.

Bullying goes beyond the actions of being rude or mean. For something to be considered bullying it needs to have two things: *intent* and *repetition*.

Intent: By intent we mean that a person who is a bully has to be aware of what they are doing and know that their behavior is causing harm to the person that they are targeting. The bully specifically engages in the behavior for the purpose of making themselves feel better by making another person feel worse.

Repetition: This behavior cannot be isolated, it must be repeated regularly to be considered bullying. A child who shoves another child and calls him a name one day would not be considered a bullying incident, rather, it is an example of an altercation and should be addressed as such. A child who shoves the same child every day and calls him names while doing so is absolutely a bully, and should be looked at differently.

How Big a Problem is Bullying?

When the topic of bullying comes up, there is almost always a person who wholeheartedly believes that bullying either is not a big problem, or that people are making too big of a deal out of it. Personally, we believe that those people may believe this because they have never experienced bullying themselves, or had a child who has experienced bullying. While that is terrific for them, there is still a multitude of statistics out there that show that many more kids do experience bullying in some way than do not. So for parents who themselves were never bullied in their adolescence and who now have children who do not experience bullying in the present time, bullying is not seen as a problem. However, for the parents with children who worry daily about getting on the school bus, who fear going to their locker because someone is waiting for them, or who are attacked verbally or physically each day at lunch, bullying is a very big deal and should be treated as the major issue we see it as.

How Effective is Bully Prevention?

In some ways, bully prevention has a tremendous benefit, but in other ways it can actually be a detriment. The reason is that without proper education, kids do not know what bullying is and neither do their parents. When a child thinks that someone throwing leaves at them when they walk home from school one day is bullying, it causes the word to lose it's power. If the term bullying is thrown out there for every minor infraction, then the word ceases to mean anything and becomes useless when we discuss it.

Another issue is that bully prevention often focuses on teaching techniques and methods that are neither realistic nor recommended by professionals. For example, the old standby of "just walk away" is perhaps the most overused and dangerous thing we can teach kids. This concept of teaching kids that if they run away from their problems they will be safe is terrible. There are times to run to escape danger, for example if your house in on fire, but running is not a coping skill, and no one can run from their problems forever. Sometimes you need to take a stand, to defend yourself, to say, "I've had enough, and this ends now!" If children have to defend themselves, whether it be through words or actions, they should be encouraged. This is why there should be a universal definition and understanding of bullying, so that children are not afraid to defend themselves for fear of being considered a bully as well. If kids are taught that they cannot speak up for themselves or defend themselves because that makes them a bully then we are failing to teach the way we should, and those kids are going to suffer for it in the long run.

Effective bully prevention begins with imparting accurate knowledge about bullying onto children. This also means that adults and educators must be well versed in the subject so they can teach, answer questions, and deal with occurrences of bullying. One of the best ways to teach bully prevention is to have set standards in order to define what is and what is not bullying, and have those standards be taught and understood by everyone in a community. It is important that everyone in the community is on board, so that children are being taught a consistent and complete message. This means that parents, teachers, and entire communities need to come together in order to develop ways to truly educate and bullyproof kids.

Bullyproof Strategies in Schools

There are many ways that schools can help bullyproof students. Talking about respect both for oneself and others is the first thing that teachers can do. Teaching kids to look a person in the eye when they speak to them is a great strategy for this because doing so also shows confidence in oneself which may lessen the likelihood of being targeted by bullies. Additionally, having an increased awareness of self-esteem training in schools is a key consideration. Teaching kids how to feel better about themselves and how to walk, talk, and act with more self-esteem is a wonderful way to create bullyproof students. Maintaining open and effective communication is a great way to encourage bullyproofing. Teaching kids that it is OK to communicate concerns with adults is important. If kids think that they will be labeled as a "tattletale" for seeking help from an adult, then they will be less likely to do so. Kids need to be taught that if someone is doing something that they should not be doing, and it is harming another student, then it is absolutely OK to seek help from a trusted adult. These things may all seem like common sense to many people reading this book, but the sad truth is that in today's society these things are not being taught.

How Martial Arts Can Help

For kids who are being bullied, martial arts can be a life changing experience. We have mentioned some key ways to help bullyproof kids in this chapter, and each and every one of these strategies can be found in a quality martial arts program. Some of the earliest lessons kids learn when they join martial arts programs are about how they carry themselves, which goes a long way in becoming bullyproof. Many kids come to their first martial arts classes without knowing things like how to walk with confidence, and to keep their head up. Many kids also do not know how to make eye contact when they speak to someone, or they do not feel comfortable doing so because they lack the self-confidence.

Martial arts helps to build the self-confidence of the individual while also nurturing self-esteem, so that kids learn about their self-worth and how they deserve to be treated. They learn to treat others with respect and in turn learn how they should expect to be treated. They learn physical self-defense, but more than that they learn about how to keep themselves safe and protected from bullying just through their actions and attitude.

In Conclusion

There are many different ways to look at bullyproofing kids, and it can be hard to filter through all the nonsense out there and decide what the best strategies really are. In our opinion it comes down to two main concepts, which are education and community. Kids need to be taught the strategies that will help them become confident and bullyproof, but they need to have these messages and lessons echoed by their whole community. The more people they hear and see these lessons from, the better chance they will have of learning them and using them. It takes a concerted effort by parents, teachers, coaches, instructors, and anyone involved in the lives of children in order to teach lasting lessons. None of us, by ourselves, can affect children's lives in a consistent and ongoing way. Together we have the best chance at making sure no child is left out, and that they all have a fair shot at being the best version of themselves - that is what we want and what must we strive for.

Jim & Tracy Hammons are the husband and wife team behind Martial Arts Advantage in Broken Arrow, Oklahoma.

Master Jim Hammons holds a 8th Degree Black Belt in Tae Kwon Do. He has been inducted into the World Martial Arts Hall of Fame, is a 3 time World Champion, and holds 18 National Champion titles. He has enjoyed teaching martial arts for over 30 years, and is a devoted husband and loving father of four. He is also a Financial Planner in South Tulsa.

Tracy Hammons is a 2nd Degree Black belt and has been training in martial arts for 16 years.

For more information visit www.martialartsadvantage.net.

CHAPTER 2:
HOW TO A.V.O.I.D. BULLYING

BY JASON WADLEY
LAKE JACKSON, TEXAS

I'm very excited to be a part of this book because, over the course of nearly four decades in the martial arts, I've seen how important it is to teach bullyproofing strategies to children and families. Here at my martial arts studio in Lake Jackson, Texas, I've dedicated my life to making sure kids have the opportunity to learn how to be safer in terms of defending themselves physically as well as mentally against anything they may face in their lives.

This is accomplished through teaching them about not only self-defense strategies, but also important life skills such as confidence and self-esteem. I'm honored to be a part of this project and to be able to share some of my thoughts on bullying.

Bullying Comes in All Forms

To have any real discussion about bullying the first thing we need to do is define it. In my experience, bullying is someone trying to force something onto someone else. This may be forcing a suggestion, an action or an impression, but it's forcibly bending another persons will in order to do something the bully wants. Bullying can be mental, physical or emotional, and there are many different avenues a bully can take. The broad idea of bullying, though, is it is one person purposefully dominating another.

Since bullying comes in so many forms, I think everyone has been exposed to it one way or another, at some point in their lives. I was bullied myself as I was going through school, and there's always someone bigger, older, tougher, mean, and just looking for someone to dominate. Even as adults we deal with bullies every day. It could be a pushy sales person, government, someone on the Internet; there are so many different things that could constitute bullying behavior. Since bullying is so prevalent, and is even all over the media, it's natural to want to seek ways to eliminate it altogether.

Can Bullying Be Eliminated?

No, it can't. I'd love to be able to say I think it's possible, but the reality is, bullying will never be completely eliminated. Unfortunately, it doesn't matter how much awareness is raised or how much we may want to completely eradicate bullying from the world because, it will always be something we have to deal with as humans.

Just take a look at the course of human history. You could stop almost anyone on the street and ask them if they like wars and the resounding answer will be no. Nobody likes wars, yet in this day and age we still have wars all over the world. It's almost unfathomable that as educated as the world is and even with the humanitarian and technological advances we still have war, genocide and the like. These things, like bullying, are a part of the makeup of human culture. People don't like it, and most of them wish we could be rid of it, but it doesn't seem a realistic goal. Instead, efforts should be made to educate people so they can bullyproof themselves and their loved ones to be protected even when faced with bullying.

Bullying in Schools

One of the most common concerns people have with bullying is how much of it occurs in schools. This is a valid concern because children spend so much of their lives in schools and parents trust they're safe while they're there. It seems there have been many changes over the last few years, though, and not all for the better.

When I was in school there seemed to be a lot of immediate discipline if bullying happened. Bullying back then was also easier to spot because whether it was verbal or physical, it was almost always visible to teachers. Nowadays, with cyber bullying and the way technology plays a role in things, bullying is different. Because of the changes in bullying, it seems there have been changes in how teachers handle it as well. School districts claim they try to educate kids about bullying and strive to stop it, but the systems they're using seem broken.

Bullyproofing Strategies That Don't Work

Before I get into the strategies I find to be the most effective, I think it's important to spend some time going over some things that, in my mind, aren't effective ways to bullyproof kids. The first is something the school systems seem to be pushing more and more, and it's the "no tolerance" policy for fighting. I don't condone fighting, but this policy doesn't make any sense when it's implemented fully. For example: two boys are in a classroom, one of the boys decides he wants to fight and starts wrestling or fighting with the other boy. If a teacher looks over and sees the two boys with their hands on each other, then both boys most likely get an in or out of school suspension depending on the school's policy.

In martial arts we actively teach our students not to fight, we teach them how to defend themselves. One is an action, one is a reaction. They're both choices that a person has to make, but those choices come from an act of aggression or an act of self-preservation and those are two very different things. However, schools don't separate them. Instead, students are taught that if they defend themselves they'll be punished the same as the person attacking them, which is a horrible message to send them. It turns them into victims who have no choices. There are, of course, other steps to take before physical altercations, but the problem is that schools don't offer any alternatives other than blanket statements and generalized consequences.

Another strategy that doesn't work is only focusing on the physical side of things. There have been so many times when a parent has brought their child in for lessons and are only focused on the physical component of self-defense because they aren't educated about how much goes into bullyproofing kids. This issue is compounded because there are actually a lot of martial arts schools out there that do only focus on fighting. Kids learn how to fight, but they don't learn any other strategies and they end up pulling the trigger early on those skills instead of using other strategies that could work instead of fighting. It all comes down to education - education for parents, for kids, for teachers and for anyone who may be involved in bullyproofing situations. Without giving someone a complete lesson on the full suite of strategies and complexities you're setting them up for failure in the long run. It's like teaching someone how to move a chess piece but not teaching them how to play the game.

Strategies That Do Work

Like I said, the most important thing is to be educated on bullying and learn about different ways to deal with it. It's easy to just throw out blanket statements and hope they work, but there's a lot more to it if we're really going to make a difference. In my years of experience the best system I've worked with so far is what I call

AVOID. This system follows what people in law enforcement know as force continuum, which is essentially a system designed to have a certain level of response based on the level of perceived threat.

In the AVOID system each letter stands for something. They are Awareness skills, Verbal skills, Offer a truce, Inform a higher authority and Defend yourself. Awareness skills means being able to recognize threats before they become dangers. Kids can learn to recognize bullies before they have an altercation, learn about how to carry themselves, the importance of whom they choose as friends and more.

Verbal skills are what to say and how to respond to a bully. These are some of the most difficult skills to really master because it takes practice and there's a lot involved such as tone, mannerisms and others. These skills also take a lot of practice, and without working on them and trying them, they won't work properly.

Offering a truce is the ability to learn to reason with a bully or any attacker. It really goes hand in hand with verbal skills because you can't offer a truce unless you know what to say and how to say it. Anyone can learn and be able to use these skills, but they have to be taught and given the opportunity to practice regularly.

Inform a higher authority means that kids have to learn that they can and should seek help if they need it. The stigma of being a tattletale is still running rampant in schools, but children need to understand that teachers and adults are allies and it's ok to seek help. In turn adults need to recognize when a child is looking for help and be able to respond appropriately.

Finally, the last step is Defending yourself. It's an important step, but it's equally important there are other options before this one is chosen. I firmly believe every human being has the right to protect themselves through words or actions and that includes kids. Defending yourself doesn't have to mean fighting, it can also mean walking away, closing a door on someone or defending with words. However, it could also mean defending with blocks or strikes. By having the force continuum of AVOID, kids have more options and are more educated. If parents and teachers all learned this same method then perhaps we'd be able to use that education to move forward in more impactful bullyproofing strategies, and get away from the equal consequences and overgeneralization of fighting.

Final Thoughts

The last thought I'd like to leave you with, is a majority of people truly believe we can get rid of bullying entirely. I think that's a wonderful idea, but it's not realistic. Bullying is an unfortunate part of our society, but it is a part of society nonetheless. Whether you find a martial arts school to enroll in for bullyproofing, or you have another resource that seems beneficial to you, I can't recommend enough to seek out that education and give your children the tools and practice necessary to use those tools. Confident, educated people are not bullied and that's what we should be working towards together.

Master Jason Wadley began his martial art training in 1980. Dedicating himself to martial arts, Master Wadley has achieved many prestigious awards and commendations.

He began training at the age of 11 under the direction of Grand Master H.U. Lee. Master Wadley continue's to train and help proliferate Taekwondo throughout the world. Master Wadley has traveled around the world teaching, training and competing.

Master Wadley's technical ability and knowledge of Taekwondo earned him the title of Technical advisor and director of training for the Unite United Taekwondo Alliance.

For more information visit www.jasonwadley.com

CHAPTER 3:
YOU CAN'T JUST IGNORE IT

BY LYNDA NELSON
BARRINGTON, NEW HAMPSHIRE

I'm thrilled to be part of the discussion about the challenges we're facing as we deal with what many people consider to be an epidemic of bullying. It's an issue all over the world, but it seems like we see and hear about it almost constantly right in our own neighborhoods. As the owner of Quest Martial Arts in Barrington, NH I've been teaching martial arts for many years and have seen many children's lives affected by bullying. I'm proud that my programs have had some truly transformational effects on many of my students, and am happy to share my thoughts here.

How Big a Problem is Bullying?

Some people out there still have the mindset that cases of bullying are "kids being kids" or similar old phrases. That mindset is a huge challenge for our society and I think it has been for a very long time. Bullying is real and its effects can be devastating to those touched by it. The continued thought process that it isn't really a problem is only going to perpetuate the problem and progress in a more negative direction moving forward. Bullying is in fact a huge problem and there are plenty of studies and statistics to love it, but if people's mindsets don't change then it will be difficult to create any positive changes.

Additionally, the advent of technology has increased the ways and frequency with which bullying can occur. Bullies don't even have to be face-to-face with their victims anymore. Words or images can be broadcast to an entire school or community in the blink of an eye and leave emotional marks that are just as painful and damaging as physical ones. Bullying is becoming easier and more widespread, and one of the first steps to dealing with a problem is admitting that there is one.

Can We Eliminate Bullying?

I don't know if it's completely possible to eliminate bullying from our lives. I'd like to think it is, but it's so prevalent and has been an issue for so long that I don't know if it's realistic to think we can. What I do know is that if we have any chance of eliminating bullying it starts with the adults. As adults we set the example and lead the way. I think that oftentimes our freedoms are misconstrued here in the United States. For example, people seem to take the idea of freedom of speech and think it means having an open invitation to say or do anything we feel like regardless of how it may affect someone else.

I think on step toward eliminating bullying is creating a culture of people who are respectful, kind, and courteous. If we had communities like this then I think we'd be able to at least minimize the quantity of incidents of bullying. I also think that education plays a key role in striving to eliminate bullying from our lives, and if people were open to learning about bullyproofing strategies then it would be beneficial to everyone.

Bullying in Schools

Parents are very often concerned with how bullying is handled in schools. This concern makes sense because kids spend the majority of their days in schools, and it's still where most bullying happens or at least originates. Parents also have cause to be concerned because the majority of schools simply don't handle bullying effectively.

I had a student one time who was being bullied in school. I met him when he was in the third grade, and found out that the same child had been bullying him consistently since kindergarten. This bully would tease him, grab him, throw him to the ground, and make fun of him and the teachers always wrote it off as "boys being boys". Anytime teachers did respond to him they'd tell him to just ignore it. Meanwhile, this innocent child was going to school everyday feeling terrible about himself because he was being harassed unrelentingly. Luckily I was able to work with this boy and his parents to resolve the issues, but it's frightening to think of how much longer the child would have had to endure the abuse if there hadn't been a change.

You Can't Just Ignore It

Although it's been the go-to response for adults to give to kids for years, telling a kid to just ignore bullying is some of the worst advice to offer - it's also the most common thing schools seem to recommend. This isn't because schools want to see kids being bullied - it's mainly because they lack the resources to offer better alternatives. Resources in this case means education and outside experts offering strategies teachers can pass on and work on with their students. Sometimes this lack of resources stems from a lack of financing, because schools think that the only way for teachers to get this important training is through a paid program. In reality there are many free, quality programs available to schools so their employees can be better prepared to combat bullying.

Again, while the advice to just ignore it has been given for years, it's not the right thing to say anymore. Bullying isn't the same as it was a few years ago never mind decades ago. Ignoring it doesn't make it go away, and it doesn't resolve any of the issues that come along with being bullied. A child can ignore a bully and walk away, but the seeds of "you're stupid, you're ugly, you're fat, you're worthless" are planted and if nothing is done they continue to grow. We need to offer strategies to children so that those words or actions of a bully never become permanent.

Strategies That Work

There are lots of different ways to help children become bullyproof. I mentioned changing the culture earlier, and I think that's a big one. In a classroom the culture has to tart from day one with a teacher making it clear what behaviors are acceptable and what behaviors aren't. Setting the tone of the culture right from the start is one way teachers can create bullyproof environments. From there they can strengthen the idea of the culture they want to promote by identifying and pointing out exceptional behavior, demonstrating the culture in their own actions, and even having guest speakers come in who will reinforce the messages. Having this type of culture also encourages students to band together as a community and rally around someone who is being picked on because they all understand what the right and wrong behavior are.

Another strategy that is successful is teaching kids about positive self-talk. This is the ability to understand that failures and mistakes aren't the end of the world, but rather are opportunities to grow and develop. It's the ability to focus on the good qualities while being able to understand and accept the bad. Positive self-talk is also a way for kids to form something of a protective bubble around themselves that can keep the negativity of others from getting to them. It's also what leads to a child having the ability to have the inner strength and confidence to look a bully in the eyes and demand to be left alone.

Toolbox Training

There isn't any one strategy that will help every child become bullyproof all of the time. Instead, it's better to consider the notion of toolbox training. Toolbox training means having multiple bullyproofing tools and strategies available to use depending on the situation. These tools include life-skills like confidence and self-esteem as well as things like posture and the ability to defend oneself. Having a toolbox at your disposal means the ability to defend against physical, mental, emotional, and social threats. It's also important to understand that no one learns how to become proficient with a tool by using it once and never touching it again - it takes practice. The road to a bullyproof world won't be quick or easy, but it will be well worth the effort.

Sensei Lynda D. Nelson is the Master Instructor and owner of the Quest Martial Arts in Barrington, New Hampshire. She has a Bachelor of Science Degree in Business Administration with a concentration in Recreation and Leisure Services. She received the Academic Award for Outstanding Achievement in her major and graduated with the highest honors. In addition to her academic awards, Ms. Nelson received First Team All-American Honors in soccer for two consecutive years.

Ms. Nelson is a 5th degree black belt in Isshin Ryu Karate. She began her martial arts training in Dover, New Hampshire at Master's Self-Defense studying Kenpo Karate. In addition to studying Kenpo Karate in Dover, she also began to study Isshin Ryu Karate in Portsmouth, New Hampshire. Her Head Instructor placed her in an accelerated martial arts training program because of her natural teaching abilities.

For more information, visit www.questmartialarts.net.

CHAPTER 4: PARENTS' ROLES IN PREVENTING BULLYING

BY CARLOS MARTIN
GOLDSBORO, NORTH CAROLINA

As the owner of Elite Athletics in Goldsboro, North Carolina, I've had the opportunity over many years of working with children and adults to see how bullying affects people differently. In my career I've trained people in martial arts and tumbling and have experienced lots of success - including multiple trips to Grand Nationals - but my biggest focus these days is child development and how to help children become bullyproof. It's a pleasure to be working with so many other professionals to bring such a tremendous resource to parents and families.

Dealing with Bullying

As a father, one of my worst fears is that my children will experience bullying in their lives. Fortunately, my three sons haven't had any issues yet and I hope that I can keep them bullyproof. I know how harmful bullying can be, not just from the stories of former and current students but also because I experienced bullying myself.

I grew up in New Jersey, and where I'm from originally wasn't the nicest area. It wasn't as bad as some other places, but there were a lot of negative influences a child could get caught up in. The older brother of my best friend bullied me and the bullying went on for a long time. In fact, it went on for years and part of the reason was that I didn't know any way to stop. I wasn't shown how to handle bullies and didn't know what options I had other than to take the abuse, so that's what I did. It certainly wasn't a great thing to have to go through, and I hope that I can help other kids avoid the same ordeals.

The Problem

Before I go any further I'd like to comment on the actual problem of bullying. Some people don't really even see it as a problem, which makes bullyproofing kids that much more difficult. In order to create solutions there needs to be admission that solutions are needed. I think that one of the things we're seeing happening now is that people try to act like it's not as big a problem as it really is, and because it gets ignored kids don't get any quality advice or instruction on how to handle it when it does happen. Kids aren't taught the first thing about being aware and they don't know what options they have when it happens, and what ends up happening is they become victims. So my first message to everyone is that bullying is in fact a problem – a big one.

Can it be Eliminated?

This is a question that I wish I had a positive answer to, but the truth is that I don't think bullying can ever truly be eliminated. It's too much a part of our society, and is present from school-aged children through adults in their careers. It's something that will probably always be around, so instead of trying to eliminate it a better option is to raise awareness about it so we can lessen it as much as possible.

I mentioned that my own children haven't been targets of bullying yet. My boys are ten, seven, and three, so the older ones have definitely reached the ages where bullying is a possibility. I think one of the main reasons they haven't been bullied is because I'm aware of the problem and take steps to make sure they're as bullyproof as possible. There are many ways to do this, but the first step is to become aware of the problem and then take steps to learn as much as you can about it.

Strategies for Parents

There are lots of different ways that parents can help their kids become bullyproof. I mentioned that awareness for the parents is important – being aware of the issues – but it's also important to teach children about awareness. Teaching children to be less naïve about their surroundings is a great thing. They can learn about what types of behaviors and crowds to avoid, and also learn to identify when someone looks like they're out for trouble. Instead of walking with their heads and eyes down they can keep their heads up and eyes forward, looking ahead and surveying their surroundings. Not only will they be able to take more in and identify potential dangers, they'll also appear more confident and so will be less likely to be targeted.

Speaking of confidence, I think another important thing is to promote confidence in your children as much as possible. In my experience I've seen time and time again that confident kids are much less likely to be bullied. They carry themselves differently and don't appear to be easy targets. Bullies tend to focus their energies on weaker people who won't give them trouble so developing true confidence in children is crucial. This can be done in lots of ways, including giving them challenges to accomplish, praising them for the good work they do, and enrolling them in activities that promote confidence. Again, this comes back to awareness and being prepared to do what you can as a parent to keep your children safe.

Another strategy that is vital is being present in your children's lives. I know that for many of us this seems like an obvious one, but it's amazing how many parents take it for granted. When I say be present in your children's lives I don't just mean be there to provide food, shelter, and affection. I mean actually be a fixture in their lives and make sure they know that you're there for them. Show up to games and events, take the time to ask them how their day is going, and don't be afraid to pry and dig deeper. Too often we're comfortable with surface answers that appease us, but we need to show our children that we're more involved than that. Ask your kids what happened at school and pay attention to how they explain things, watch for warning signs, and make sure they know that they can talk to you about anything. This active dedication to being present in kids' lives is one of the best ways to take steps toward keeping them bullyproof.

Things That Don't Work

While I think that being present in your children's lives is very important, there's a difference between being an active parent and being a BFF. I think that these days, maybe because of the effects of social media, parents are more worried about being friends with their kids than being parents. As a parent I know it's a hard struggle to keep a balance we feel comfortable with, and for many of us we want to do things differently than our own parents, but we have to be careful not to cross the line. A relationship with a parent is not, and should not, be the same as with a friend. Parents are there to protect and comfort in different ways than a friend is, and kids need to know that they have parents who are looking out for them.

Another strategy that's ineffective is giving kids the advice to immediately defend themselves physically regardless of the situation. The advice to stand up for themselves without any other options or training is impractical, and it's not something that they'll be able to use in the long run. We also don't want to raise our own bullies, and telling them that it's ok to always meet aggression with more aggression or violence with more violence is very narrow-minded and can lead to more issues. Instead we need to provide ongoing training that will be effective because it gives a variety of options and techniques.

Final Advice

The topics of bullying and bullyproofing are immense and can't be completely condensed to one chapter, but I hope I've given you some tips and advice that you can take with you. My final advice is to confront the beast of bullying and face it head-on. Don't be afraid to have those conversations with your kids so you know what's going on. From there you can develop strategies and seek advice from others to help your bullyproofing efforts, and even be proactive in your bullyproofing. With a healthy balance of parental involvement along with providing tools and options to kids about bullying we can work together to help raise awareness and lessen bullying's ugly effects.

Carlos Martin is the owner and instructor of Elite Athletics and Elite Martial Arts in Goldsboro, North Carolina.

Carlos began his martial arts training in 1987 and Martin currently holds a 6th degree black belt in American Tae Kwon Do Moo Duk Kwan. He has competed on the local and national karate circuits, winning various titles and championships.

Carlos also led his All-Star Cheerleading Team at Elite Athletics to numerous championships over the years, and now brings that elite-level training to the recreational tumbling student.

For more information, visit www.goldsboroelite.com

CHAPTER 5:
WHY BULLIES BULLY

BY MARK JOHNSON
SIGNAL MOUNTAIN, TENNESSEE

As the owner and instructor of Tiger Rock Martial Arts in Signal Mountain, Tennessee I've spent many years working with youth and adults in my community. I've been a martial artist for nearly thirty years and have earned the rank of 7th degree black belt in my organization, and my experience has allowed me to see how important an issue bullying is to address. It really is something that affects nearly everyone in some way at some time, and I'll be sharing my own ideas about the topic here. It's a passion of mine to help as many kids as possible become bullyproof, and I think this book series is a terrific thing to be a part of in order to help continue spreading the message.

Is Bullying Really a Problem?

As funny as that question may sound to some people reading this, it's actually a question I get asked sometimes. The people who ask it aren't necessarily trying to be rude – they just may be a part of the incredibly small percentage of people who haven't experienced bullying themselves or with a loved one. However, anyone who has been bullied themselves or who has had friends or family members who have been bullied knows firsthand how much of a problem bullying can be.

Personally, I was bullied throughout school when I was younger and I still remember how bad it felt. For me the worst bullying happened when I was in middle school, around the time I was ten years old. I had a lot of health problems growing up and when I was ten years old I only weighed about thirty-five pounds. Elementary school wasn't so bad, but once I got to middle school I was picked on pretty mercilessly for being small and also being different. I also had a tracheotomy tube in my throat, so to the bullies I was a kid who looked different and seemed like an easy target. For someone who's never been bullied themselves it may be easy to shrug their shoulders and say it's not a big deal, but for people like me who have been through the torment of bullying it's absolutely a large issue that needs to be addressed.

Bullying in Schools

For me bullying happened in school, and I know this is also the case for many other kids. School is someplace where kids obviously spend a lot of their time so it makes sense that bullying incidents are commonplace there. On top of that, schools have a limited number of teachers and a large number of students. As the grade levels get higher, class sizes usually get bigger, and teachers have even more students to keep track of. Additionally, the schools typically get larger as the grades go up and that means there are more places bullying can happen out of sight from adults. This doesn't mean that teachers aren't doing their jobs. On the contrary, I truly believe that most teachers do everything they can to take care of their students, but it's a difficult situation for them. That being said, I do think there are some strategies teachers can use to help minimize bullying.

First, I think teachers need to take the time to really listen carefully to their students. Sometimes it does seem like teachers have the "things just happen" mentality, and maybe don't see problems as big as they are to the child who's being affected. I think communication is key, and teachers who take the time to really understand what's going on in their students' lives will have more success in keeping bullying issues under control. I can say that when I was bullied as a kid I didn't want to tell my parents about it because I was embarrassed, but I wish there had been a teacher or someone I could go to talk about what was happening. In order to get there, though, students need to feel like their teachers care about them and that's done through better communication.

Along those same lines, I think that teachers who can communicate effectively and listen to their students have a better chance of identifying and eliminating bullying issues early. I like to use the analogy of comparing bullying to a wildfire. If someone flicks a cigarette with a little spark it may not look like much, but if that spark hits some dry grass then you've got a flame started. Reacting quickly to that little flame means catching it before it gets out of control and stifling it, but if you were to ignore that flame and let it grow then eventually it would continue spreading and become much more difficult to contain or eliminate. I see bullying in much the same way. Sometimes I think teachers might let small behaviors go because they're choosing their battles, but when they do that the lines aren't clearly drawn. Pretty soon the behaviors escalate, bullying begets bullying, and it becomes like the wildfire. You don't wait until the Smoky Mountains are on fire before you call the fire department - you take care of that little flame before it has a chance to spread.

I think there are lots of ways teachers can stop the spread of bullying. Communication is one of them, of course. Another thing teachers can do is to educate their students as much as possible about bullying while their also teaching their regular subjects. When I say educate I mean give students specific instruction about what bullying is, what it looks like, how it will be handled, and steps that will be taken if it happens. Creating this kind of environment where everyone is on the same page can really go a long way in setting kids up to be bullyproof and feel safe in school.

What Doesn't Work?

Anytime we look at strategies that work I think it's a good idea to look at some popular strategies that don't work as well. There are lots of different things people try to do with good intentions, but the reality is that some of these methods cause more harm than good. One of these methods is the "zero tolerance" policy that a lot of schools have implemented. This policy essentially means that if something happens then everyone is in trouble – the bully, the child being bullied, and maybe even people who were around the incident when it happened. It's almost like we're treating everyone involved like a criminal and like they've done something wrong, and not only is this mentality harmful to the victim of bullying but also to the bully.

Bullies aren't criminals, yet many times we assume their "bad kids" because of their behavior. I think that's a mistake because the majority of bullying happens as a result of the bully having some kind of issues on their own lives. We may not know their full story, and we'll never know what's causing the bullying behaviors unless we take the time to find out. Creating "zero tolerance" policies only succeeds in pushing kids further away rather than helping them improve their situations. At the end of the day we're talking about children here, and they all deserve a chance to be happy and safe – it might take more effort and understanding on our part, though.

Why Bullies Bully

It's one thing to say we should try understanding bullies better, but putting that into practice is another thing altogether. I think it might help if we could identify specific reasons why bullies engage in bullying behavior, but the truth is there isn't any single answer. I think that many times bullying is a result of learned behavior, and perhaps bullies have been bullied by someone close to them in their own lives. They may be being abused by a parent or older sibling, or see someone being abused and bullying others is their way to cope with it.

I also think that bullies often engage in those behaviors for attention. Again, it might be because of bigger issues in their lives, but for some reason they need the attention that bullying gives them and they seek it out. For those types of kids negative attention is better than no attention, and that may be why the behavior continues even after repercussions. Unfortunately there's no blanket statement or explanation for why bullies bully, but as adults and educators it's our job to do what we can to figure out the underlying reason and do what we can to help that child.

Advice for Parents

Being a martial arts instructor I've worked with hundreds of kids who have been bullied before they came to train or who actually wanted to join because of bullying. Over the years I've seen some things that I think work really well for parents who are trying to bullyproof their kids. The first and most important thing is to keep the lines of communication open with your kids. Make sure they know that they can talk to you about anything and that you won't judge them for it. Kids have to feel safe to open up, and it should be an ongoing process where you ask them how things are and have real conversations with them about their lives and what's happening. Having good communication will help you to find out about bullying issues before they become out of control, and will also give you key information about how to proceed. For example, something as simple as finding out what kind of bullying is happening is very important. How you help your child handle bullying on the soccer field, at school, online, or someplace else can look very different, require different strategies, and involve different people.

Another great way parents can help bullyproof their kids is by giving them different strategies. Different types of bullying require different strategies, but some strategies can be useful in a variety of situations. One of the reasons that martial arts is such a great bullyproofing tool is because we teach those types of strategies in every class. Of course we teach kids how to defend themselves physically, but the mental self-defense is even more important. Self-esteem and confidence are qualities that once taught are able to permeate one's entire existence. Children who develop these life skills are able to walk with their heads held high and exude an air of someone who isn't an easy target. We're all part of the animal kingdom, and bullies are like predators who seek out easy targets. If your child is walking with that confidence in their eyes and body language then they're instantly less likely to be picked on. Martial arts uses different drills and lessons in every class that help to build up those life skills, and learning those skills is what ultimately helped me to overcome bullying in my own life as a child.

Taking Action

When you look at bullying and how terrible it can be for everyone involved, you might wonder if we can ever eliminate it completely. I'm really not sure if that's a possibility, but it's like anything else in life. If you want something you've got to take action to create change. If you're as passionate as I am about keeping kids bullyproof and maybe even eliminating bullying altogether I encourage you to continue seeking information about it. Find people in your community who are likeminded and see what you're able to do in your circle of influence, and then watch as that influence is able to grow and involve others. I've spent much of my life combating bullying, and while it's not always easy I can promise you that it's certainly work worth doing.

Mark Johnson is the owner and instructor at Tiger Rock Martial Arts of Signal Mountain, Tennessee. Born and raised in the Chattanooga area, Mark has been teaching for 22 years and specializes in teaching young students.

For more information visit www.markjohnsontkd.com

CHAPTER 6: CONFIDENCE VS. COCKINESS

BY RUSSELL WRIGHT
ALEXANDER CITY, ALABAMA

As the owner and instructor of United Martial Arts in Alexander City, Alabama, I've always been driven to help kids become safer by teaching them about being bullyproof. I've been training in the martial arts for many years, earning the rank of 7th degree black belt, and throughout all of my training I've seen countless examples of kids being bullied and needing help to deal with what's happening. Because of the prevalence of bullying, I've made it one of my life's missions to help protect the youth of my city by helping them to truly become bullyproof.

My Experience With Bullying

Many people have stories about their own experiences with bullying and I'm no exception. When I was a child I moved around a lot because of my mom's job, sometimes every year or two. Because of the frequent moves I was constantly the new kid in town and had to try to make new friends. I was also overweight, so you can imagine how things went for me sometimes for being the new, fat kid in a new town with no friends.

Bullying affected me in ways that stayed with me for years, and even today I remember the experiences. I remember trying different strategies to stop the bullying, and never knowing what I could do to end the cycle. Often times I ended up doing things that just made the bullying worse. I tried to be the class clown, make friends with bullies, ignore the things they said and did, and even became a bully myself at one point as a defense mechanism. I figured it was better to join them than be attacked by them, but that only made me feel worse because I was helping to do to other kids what I was trying to avoid for myself.   Eventually I was able to learn how to be comfortable and confident in my own skin, and those lessons changed the direction of my entire life. I'm grateful for the positive influences that helped me to get where I am today, and hope my words offer some helpful insight to those reading this book.

How Bad Is Bullying?

If you're not being bullied, have never been bullied, and have never had a loved one experience bullying then you may not understand how bad bullying is. There's a small percentage of people that this is true for, but for the vast majority of people they have experienced bullying in some way over the course of their lives. It's different when you experience something firsthand because you can speak to the effect it has on your life, and it enhances your ability to have compassion for others. Bullying is indeed a terrible problem we're facing in society and it's effects are long-lasting and far reaching.

For those of you who may not understand why bullying is such a big problem we're facing right now and maybe have the attitude that kids complaining about bullying should just "toughen up", one of the things you must understand is that bullying isn't the same now as it was when you were growing up. When we were kids bullying usually meant getting pushed around at school or made fun of either at school or on the bus. Once we were home we were in our safe zone, where the schoolyard bullies couldn't reach us. These days bullying knows no boundaries and can follow kids anywhere they go. Social media has morphed bullying into an insurmountable beast to battle against, and this beast can reach kids twenty-four hours a day and seven days a week. Traditional bullying still exists, as well, but now we've got the added threat of cyber-bullying where kids can be harassed and ridiculed anywhere they go. These messages or rumors spread on social media can burn through an entire class in the blink of an eye, leaving an even more indelible mark on the psyche of the person being bullied.

Keys to Combat Bullying

As I said, bullying has changed quite a bit over the years. In the past bullying was usually more physical and the way to defend yourself was a little more clear cut. With the advent of online bullying we can still use similar strategies, but we have to take a closer look at what methods work best and how they can be properly implemented. The first thing we need to realize is that there is never going to be a quick fix or magic method that works every time for every situation. Instead, there are going to be different strategies for different situations, and it's important to give kids the opportunity to learn and practice these different strategies so they can be ready to choose the appropriate one when the time comes.

One major key to combating bullying that is instrumental to a good foundation of bullyproofing is to build confidence and learn what internal and external confidence are. Having confidence in oneself is a great way to defend against any kind of bullying whether it be mental or physical, and confidence is something that can spread to all areas of a person's life once they have it and are displaying it proudly. Internal confidence means feeling good about yourself on the inside and knowing your own self-worth. Too often I see kids who don't think they have any value or think they deserve to be treated poorly for some reason. Having internal confidence and a sense of self-worth ensures that those feelings of insecurity don't take over.

External confidence is what happens to a person's demeanor once the internal confidence has been built up. When a person has external confidence they walk with their heads up, their eyes forward, and with a sense of purpose. External confidence is immediately recognized by others, and the person who is exuding that sense of confidence in themselves instantly becomes less of a target. We need to remember that we're all part of the animal world, and the predator vs. prey mentality is very real. Think of a bully like a lion stalking it's prey, and the other kids like water buffalo. The lion isn't going to go after the alpha of the water buffalo group, it's going to go after one that looks weaker for an easier target. Bullies will do this almost every time because they don't want to mess with the kid who will give them problems, they want the kid who will take the beating or abuse and not defend themselves.

Confidence Isn't Cockiness

While confidence is an essential ingredient to a bullyproof life, it's important to differentiate between confidence and cockiness. While adults typically recognize the difference fairly easily, kids may have a more difficult time separating the two because they can be similar. One main difference is that confident people don't act like they have anything to prove to others. They don't saunter up to strangers with their chest puffed out and say, "Let me show you how tough I am." Confident people don't need to do things like that because they feel the confidence in themselves and don't have an urge to prove anything to anyone else. Confident people are comfortable with who they are, while cocky people have insecurities and still struggle with the need to prove their worth or abilities to others.

Things That Don't Work

I've given some basic outlines of strategies that work to help bullyproof kids, but there are also a number of strategies that just don't work. For example, the idea that "sticks and stones may break my bones but names will never hurt me" is ridiculous. I think it must have been a bully that came up with that little gem because of course words can hurt! Words can cut deeper than physical pain sometimes, and can also leave scars that last forever. To dismiss a bully being terrible and hurtful to another child by offering this empty rhyme unfairly marginalizes the feelings of the person being bullied.

Another thing that simply doesn't work is the implementation and enforcement of "zero tolerance" policies. These policies just don't make any sense to me and I've seen how much damage they can actually do. I've had students in my martial arts school who have told me they stood there and allowed themselves to get abused because they didn't want to get suspended for defending themselves, and I've had administrators tell me that "it takes two to tango" when discussing the issue. That's absurd! It's just absurd that if one kid is attacking another the right thing to do, according to these policies, is for the kid getting hit to take the abuse. If the kid being attacked pushes, blocks, or touches the other kid in any way while attempting to defend themselves then they're seen as equally at fault. What lesson is that teaching? No lesson that I agree with, that's for sure. It's promoting a victim mentality that I just can't agree with, and I can't help but see it as doing much more harm than good.

A Baseball Metaphor

I like to use a baseball metaphor when I'm describing my approach to bullyproofing strategies. First base is avoid or ignore. A child who is being bullied can start off by avoiding any areas where the bully may be, especially areas where there aren't any other friends or adults around. If this doesn't work and the bully still tries to go after them, a kid can try ignoring the bullying behavior. By choosing to ignore the bully a child is able to feel empowered for making the decision and this might also aid in confidence building.

Second base is trying to talk to the bully. This may be difficult, but I've seen some great examples of a kid using "verbal judo" to diffuse a situation. For example, if a bully comes up and acts like they're going to get rough then the victim can explain that if they start fighting they'll both get in trouble and it wouldn't be worth it. There are different variations here, but essentially it's a matter of the kid getting bullied being able to talk their way out of the situation. It's not an easy strategy, but a child who's also been working on confidence building will have an advantage here.

Third base is seeking out and talking to an authority figure. It could be a principal, teacher, guidance counselor, or anyone else in the school seen as an authority. It's important that kids don't feel like seeking help from these people is a form of tattling, because that will only hurt their confidence and discourage them from seeking this important help. Rather, kids should be taught early and often that if they need help they should find a person they trust to confide in.

If none of these strategies work then the person being bullied has gone around the bases and needs to defend home plate. This means that if they're still being bullied and nothing else has helped, they must defend themselves. While this is the last option, it's one that I stand by wholeheartedly. No one has a right to put their hands on you and cause you harm - it's called assault and it's not ok. If a child has tried to handle things by using the strategies I explained and they're still being attacked then I strongly feel that they have a right to protect themselves. This, of course, clashes with the zero tolerance policies that many schools have, but it's how I feel.

Final Thoughts

There are lots of ways parents can help their kids become bullyproof, and this is really just the tip of the iceberg. If I were to give parents some final advice for how to bullyproof their kids I'd say that you've got to instill the sense of self-worth early and consistently. Make sure you're child knows that they have value and no one should be able to make them feel any different. Also, be involved in your children's lives. The more involved you are the more likely you are to know about issues when they come up, and your kids will be more likely to open up to you if you're consistently talking to them about what's going on in their lives. This also lets you pay attention to what's happening in their social environment. You can't track and monitor them all day every day, but you can keep an eye on the type of crowd they're spending time with and make sure it's a group of friends that are good for your kids. Bullying may be unavoidable, but by taking the time to learn about and use some key strategies you're taking a big step toward creating a bullyproof generation.

Russell Wright is the owner and instructor at United Arts Training center. Opened in 1990, United Arts Training Center has been serving Alexander City and the surrounding communities.

Master Russell Wright created a martial arts studio based in Lissajous Do Ryu under Grandmaster Roy Williams, but also encompassing styles from many masters, such as Tae Kwon Do and Judo under Grandmaster Dana Rhodes, and Kickboxing under Grandmaster Joe Lewis, along with Non-Deadly Force and Last Resort Tactics under Senior Tactical Master Tom Patire. This idea of combining and mixing styles into one all-encompassing system became the source for the name United Arts.

For more information, visit www.unitedarts.us.

CHAPTER 7: WHY MOST "ANTI-BULLY" PROGRAMS DON'T WORK

BY JOHN NOTTINGHAM
PHOENIX, ARIZONA

Bullying is an important issue to me. So important, actually, that my entire career could be said to have begun as a result of bullying. I own and operate USA Martial Arts in Phoenix, Arizona, and I love what I do. One of the primary reasons I started in martial arts was that I was bullied as a kid, and I understand that feeling of powerlessness. Participating in martial arts changed my life so much that I now devote myself to sharing anti-bullying strategies with others. My training and experience have culminated in a program I call "Bullyproof Vest", which is based on effective, common-sense practices (even though they are probably contrary to many of the mainstream views currently being advocated).

Is Bullying Really a Big Deal?

The short answer is, yes, of course it is! However, I do realize that some people think bullying really isn't that big of a problem. They say kids just need to suck it up or that people just need to be tougher. But this mentality does not address the struggle that many children face every day as they are taunted, intimidated, and even threatened by those society would call "bullies". It certainly doesn't equip them to respond to the problem effectively. I believe bullying is not only harmful to the person being bullied, it's damaging to the perpetrator as well. Bullying is also detrimental to society as a whole and has been around since the beginning of human existence. We need to do what we can to combat it, and I believe the best approach is to empower individuals as opposed to implementing the current school-wide anti-bullying programs.

Anti-Bullying Programs Don't Work

The sweeping, school-wide anti-bullying programs don't work, and this has been proven through several major scientific studies. Part of the problem lies in the way people have been taught to think about bullying and the programs that go along with it. First, bullying isn't a clinical diagnosis (although many are now attempting to make it so) but rather a social label. This is ironic because many in the anti-bullying movement say it's wrong to name-call, and yet here we are redirecting the name-calling back at the bully -- it just doesn't make sense!

Anti-bullying isn't the first example, but rather another in a long line of ill-conceived programs that have had the opposite result of what was intended. For example, the DARE program (Drug Awareness Resistance Education), was a target-specific program designed to keep kids off drugs. Billions of tax dollars were thrown down this well-intentioned hole, and we now have long-term studies that show that some schools with strong DARE programs actually had increases in drug sales and use.

Another example is a program that put fear in the hearts of an entire generation of kids: Stranger Danger. This program taught kids that all strangers were bad and should be avoided. There's the story of the lost little boy in Utah who was passed several times by rescuers because he was hiding from the strangers he saw. He thought he was in danger from the very people who were there to rescue him! We terrified a generation of children and their parents by promoting fear of things that were unlikely to happen instead of educating them about real risk factors. We know that non-familial abductions are extremely rare, yet it has become a pervasive thought for parents. Even today the lingering effects of Stranger Danger keep parents from letting their kids go to the park or participate in certain activities. In reality these activities would make them safer, because when we learn to participate in calculated risk we learn how to better mitigate risk and unintended consequences. Social scientists and psychologists tell me that children who are taught how to participate in risk are safer, happier and more successful because they better understand how to calculate it. Unfortunately, this approach is the opposite of that taken by many national programs.

What is Happening in Bullying Efforts Today

These programs, along with anti-bullying programs, haven't worked mainly because they focus on the wrong things: victim culture, division, reporting on others, blaming, abdicating safety, and acting powerless. My issue with victim culture is that it robs children of their power and dignity and leaves them at risk for more abuse in the future. The combination of denial, blame and powerlessness is never a good defensive strategy - nor is it a happy way to live life.

Instead of creating solutions, what we create are even more complex problems than what we had to begin with. Today bullying is obviously a hot button issue, but it's often politically motivated. It isn't truly focused on getting measurable results, but is more of a feel-good movement. To get real results we have to be honest about bullying, but the programs being developed are not responding correctly to the reports we are receiving on the matter.

A great way to prove the political motivation of the current anti-bullying movement is to comment against it. You know what happens when you do? You get bullied! You're not allowed to disagree with the Establishment, because they're focused on this mission of eliminating bullying that's driven more by profits and politics than it is by science and facts. What we need to do is bring some realistic and practical thinking into the conversation so we can address the real problem instead of just trying to make ourselves feel better about it.

I don't doubt everyone's motives. Most people truly care and want to make a difference. I believe their hearts are in the right place, and I have the utmost respect for those who have been doing the hard work all these years to build resilience and self-esteem in children. But when it comes to programs to improve the wellbeing of our children, we need to be sure that our efforts are moving us in the right direction. I observed the multi-billion-dollar waste of money that was the DARE program, and I saw a generation of scared mothers and children because of the alarmism of Stranger Danger. The current anti-bullying movement smells the same to me. Again, billions of dollars are being spent on programs that aren't focusing on the right areas and are instead creating more complex problems.

Change the Focus

I've mentioned that we need to change the focus and ask the right questions; we need to change the way we think about bullying. I love to tell a story about Mother Teresa, someone you can't help but hold up as an extraordinary example of love and compassion. In this story, Mother Teresa was in a meeting, and there were anti-war protests happening in the streets near her. One of the protestors came running up to her and said, "Mother Teresa, how could you be here in this meeting? We need you with us at the anti-war rally!" Mother Teresa calmly said to the man, "Call me when it's a peace rally."

I think that's a pretty profound way to express the power that comes with a change in thinking. That's what the anti-bullying movement needs. Right now the thinking is mostly focused on victims. The anti-bullying movement highlights victims, and so that's what we see covered by the media. We also see this approach turning those victims into anti-heroes and attention-getters. Let's remember for a moment that almost every school mass-murderer has seen himself as a victim. People have the ability to commit horrible atrocities when they justify themselves as victims. We're focused on the wrong things and using the wrong methods to protect our kids. The result has been nothing short of catastrophic.

The Wrong Way to Bullyproof a Child

There are many wrong methods that different bullyproofing programs use, and I'll highlight a couple of them here. One strategy on the anti-bullying front essentially turns peers into informants, creating further division among students in schools. This method says, 'we have to have our bystanders tell on the bully'. In other words, 'we need to have kids reporting on everyone else'. This requires teachers to operate as police. So great! The outcome is totalitarianism and that's what we're teaching our children. Instead of giving them strategies that might be more difficult – but work! – we're content to take the easy way out and abdicate responsibility to other kids and teachers. Blame is at the foundation of the anti-bully movement and alarmism is one of its most pervasive tools. It makes it convenient to then blame teachers and school administrators when things go wrong. The result? More division, more blame, more conflict, and attorneys profiteering with lawsuits.

Other 'big ideas' include hanging up lots of anti-bullying posters, or holding big assemblies with clowns and magicians and whatever celebrity is focusing on bullying issues that week. All of these various programs drain taxpayer money and only make us feel good about taking action when in reality we're not doing anything substantial or lasting. We even have a conflict of interest when we maintain zero-tolerance policies while simultaneously trying to teach kids about tolerance. How can you teach tolerance with zero-tolerance policies at the forefront of current strategy?

The Right Way to Bullyproof a Child

In order to bullyproof kids properly, we need to change the foundation of the entire anti-bullying movement. Our focus must be on peace training, kindness training and character education.

The first step in changing the foundation of the whole approach is to start teaching kids how to put things in context. Children lack the ability to do that and therefore we need to help them. We need to teach them how to understand their feelings, and that compassion and empathy are important. This isn't a quick fix – and it's not going to come from a poster – but it's important for kids to know that words and ideas aren't always permanent judgment. We don't want to permanently label a person a bully, or believe that we're permanently labeled ourselves, but rather we should foster things like forgiveness, understanding and compassion. Of course there is the reality of having to deal with aggression or physical bullying when it happens, and there are tools for that too, but it begins with teaching kids how to love, be tolerant and establish mutual respect.

Bullyproof Strategies

One of the ways we can impart these ideas at the most fundamental level is to teach boundary-setting, which is a critical life skill. If we don't teach kids about boundaries when they're young, we set them up for a lifetime of failure. We overprotect them, we coddle them, and we feel good about the protection we give, but we don't teach them how to protect themselves by creating boundaries and understanding how they work. I know adults who are highly educated, but who are also completely derelict in this area. They have no ability to protect themselves from bullying behaviors – and it goes all the way up to the corporate level.

It all begins by setting boundaries, owning our own mental and physical space, and learning that others have the right to their opinions and space as well. We don't always have to agree with everyone, but can't we have non-adversarial discussions? We can disagree without being disagreeable and teach our kids about boundary setting in the process. This is a radical shift from the rhetoric of the current anti-bullying movement.

Part of mental boundary-setting is teaching kids that their value doesn't come from other people. Right now we have a generation of kids that has been told that words can destroy them. I would never want my children to believe that words can destroy who they are, because that puts all of the power into other people's opinions about them. Instead, we can allow other people to have their opinions and we have the option to reject them. It's OK for somebody else to have a different opinion and we can know that it doesn't have to affect us. Maybe they're having a horrible day or maybe they have a horrible life, but our value doesn't lie in someone else's opinion of us. The pervasive message of the anti-bullying movement is the opposite: that we have to somehow control how others perceive us (as if we could even do that). We shouldn't even try to control the perceptions of others lest we risk becoming bullies ourselves! It's a dangerous road to go down, and therefore it is not a methodology I advocate.

Different Courses of Action

The approach we take in our anti-bullying program at USA Martial Arts is to teach kids that their personal value and the way they perceive themselves should never be wrapped up in someone else's opinion of them, and I've got a great way to demonstrate how different this approach is from a typical anti-bullying program. There's a popular demonstration that people do in assemblies or classrooms where the presenter has students write down horrible insults on a piece of paper. The presenter assists by giving them ideas for nasty, horrible things they could say to others and then has the kids crumple up the paper. Next, the kids are told to uncrumple the paper and flatten it back out, the point being that the wrinkles or scars from the words are still there and that they can never be taken back.

What a harmful message to send to children – that they are permanently damaged or scarred from someone saying something negative about them. This approach is exactly what the current anti-bullying movement is all about, though. Current "experts" are capitalizing on a victim culture, creating kids who see themselves as injured and permanently wounded from these offensive words.

What we do instead is a similar exercise, but I use a $20 bill instead of plain paper. I insult it, yell at it, crunch it, wad it up, rub it in my armpit, step on it, and all kinds of ridiculous things. Then I hold it up and ask who still wants it. Some kids initially say, "eww, gross!" But as soon as I tell them they can take this $20 right now and go spend it, the hands shoot up to take it. I say, 'But I was horrible to this $20 bill! I said terrible things to it, I stepped all over it…why do you still want it?' The kids want it because it still works - it still has value even though it went through some tough stuff. I explain to them that their value works the same way: their inherent value never changes because they get roughed up or bad things happen to them. Carl Jung said, "I am not what happened to me. I am what I choose to become". This offers hope and healing. To me, that's a much better message to be teaching our kids.

Giving Them the Tools

The tools we give to our children need to actually work, not just make us feel good as parents and educators. The goal of our anti-bullying program is to teach children how to stay soft on the inside – kind, compassionate, understanding, and forgiving – but also to carry the tools they need to protect themselves. This empowers them to put on their "Bullyproof Vest", so when insults come their way they bounce right off. The main focus is to build their confidence, self-esteem, and sense of self-worth above all. By doing this we're able to create a mindset in our kids that they can't control other people's thoughts, but they absolutely can control their own.

Our students learn these skills through instruction, role-playing and practice. It's no different than teaching kids about fire safety and practicing what to do in an emergency. By focusing on skills that work and empower our kids, they gain abilities that can protect them from bullying. We may not be able to stop kids from getting picked on, but we can train them and give them the tools to respond appropriately. We can teach kids to retain their personal value and walk away from the situation without feeling like they surrendered their dignity. The anti-bullying movement promotes blame and powerlessness. It's the message that you cannot protect yourself and that others must always come to your rescue. It is devoid of problem-solving skills, responsibility, dignity and most importantly common-sense safety. Right now we're telling kids that they don't have any inherent value apart from the opinions of other people. We teach them to walk away without feeling right about it, or to rat out other kids immediately. What ends up happening is that the kids being bullied still feel terrible and now they are also being ostracized. Worse yet, they become "heroes" of a sort that focuses on glorifying the art of victimization – and the gruesome cycle continues. It can equate to a social death, and time and again, I have seen the way it damages self-esteem.

We have to give kids the tools to become bullyproof, and part of that is changing the victim mentality. We have a victim-centric culture now that is perpetuated by the current anti-bullying movement. Let's change the focus from victim to hero. We put kids in a program and build their confidence. They start standing taller; they engage people and make eye contact; and they are able to communicate non-verbally that they are not an easy target. They no longer fit the victim profile - they become a hero. Best of all, these skills and dignity and resilience can stay with them for life. This hero culture is what we want to continue developing, because a hero does what's right. A hero takes what he has learned and continues to spread those skills, even to the point of standing up for people who can't stand up for themselves. She has the guts to go sit down with the kid who is all alone at lunch, or to stand up for the kid who's not being invited to play at recess. That's hero culture! You don't get that by making heroes out of victims but rather by making heroes out of heroes – out of people exhibiting the behavior you want to see more of. That's what we should be encouraging through the tools and strategies we give our kids.

A Word on Bullies

By now you've got a pretty good idea that my views and methods are a bit contrarian to others with which you might be familiar. I'd also like to offer a different way to think about bullies themselves. Right now the main method of bully prevention is essentially bully-hunting. I've been teaching child safety for a long time, and my biggest concern with bully-hunting is what would be found if we were to dig deeper into bullying behaviors. A major indicator of an abused child is, in fact, the displaying of bullying behaviors. Many times these kids are getting bullied at home and then they go to school and bully others. It's a mistake to throw the baby out with the bathwater; it's a tragedy to write off these kids as "bullies" without trying to help them. The children who are labeled as bullies may be the ones who need us most because they have no one else advocating for them. If we start throwing people away, how can we hope to help them?

Bullying is an issue that we all must be aware of in order to combat it. I want to encourage everyone to take a step back and think about bullying in a different way. While the methods out there now are well-meaning, I think we're being taught to focus on the wrong things and ask the wrong questions. We owe it to our kids to take responsibility and prepare them for the world as effectively as possible. We need to create a hero culture instead of a victim culture.

To wrap it all up, love your children enough to teach them how to be resourceful problem solvers. Help them develop their social and emotional intelligence by empowering them with the ability to set personal boundaries. Teach them that their self-worth does not come from the opinions of others. They are valuable all on their own and they are worth protecting.

John Nottingham is the founder, President and Technical Director of USA Martial Arts in Phoenix, AZ. He was honored with the distinguished title "Master" in 1997. Master Nottingham, a 7th Degree Black Belt, was inducted into the International Hall of Fame on July 23, 2005. He holds multiple advanced degrees of Black Belt and numerous teaching credentials and certifications.

John developed the BullyProof Vest Program as a response to "anti-bully" programs that were proven ineffective. The BullyProof Vest program was developed as a peace process rather than the typical punitive process. Built on a foundation of bodyguard concepts, John Nottingham's BullyProof Vest program integrates elements of advanced threat assessment, effective boundaries, self defense, verbal judo, social and emotional intelligence.

For more information visit www.usa-martialarts.com

CHAPTER 8: CYBER-BULLYING — THE NEXT GENERATION OF BULLYING

BY BRETT LECHTENBERG
SANDY, UTAH

Over the years I've established myself as one of Utah's number one authorities in personal safety. My deepest passion lies in working with families to train them in strategies to stay safe in all aspects of their lives. I've taught a number of personal protection programs for children and adults, and one of the most common concerns families have is the issue of bullying. Bullying is one of the biggest topics we hear about these days. It's permeated our culture, existing not only in face-to-face incidents but also digitally. With the prevalence of things like social media and text messaging, cyber bullying is running rampant more than ever and families need to be aware of the issue as well as strategies to combat it.

What is Cyber Bullying?

People may have varying ideas of what bullying is. Personally, I define bullying as any repeated act from one person towards a target that causes that target to feel harassed, shamed, fearful of physical danger, or anything along those lines. Essentially bullying is generally an unwanted action by a person or persons, usually repeated more than once, that keeps a target in some sort of negative position.

Many people will immediately read those definitions and picture a schoolyard bully picking on other children. That's certainly a common form of bullying, but by no means the only one. In these technology driven days another form of bullying, known as cyber bullying, is increasing at an alarming rate. Generally, cyber bullying is very similar to physical bullying in its core definition. It's harassment or intentional embarrassment through some form of electronic medium like Facebook, Twitter, YouTube videos, Flickr images, etc. The difference is that there is no physical confrontation. The bullying is electronic, but it's still a repeated act of negative action towards a target.

Although not everyone is even aware of it, the reality is that cyber bullying is becoming the most dangerous and common type of bullying. One reason is that cyber bullying never goes away. A child may be in school for six hours a day, but cyber bullying doesn't have to happen at school. Actually, in my own opinion and from my research, cyber bullying doesn't really happen much at school. At school they tell the kids to turn their cell phones off. They also have limited access to computers, and the access they do have is typically monitored and in a structured environment. After school, though, is where we see the most problems. This is when kids have free access to their phones, tablets, computers, etc. If they decide they want to make a target out of someone, they can just sit and do it all day and all night if they like. It's a much bigger, scary, and more dangerous animal than "traditional" bullying.

Effects of Cyber Bullying

The effects of bullying on anyone, child or adult, can be devastating. However, most adults reach a stage in their lives where the opinions of others are a lot less important to them. They figure, "I've got a few good friends, that's great. I don't care about everybody else". Most kids don't have that same sense of self-esteem. They want to be liked, they want to be accepted. They want to be part of the cool social circle and "in" crowd, so when bullying happens it's very damaging to them. Kids, much more so than adults, are really affected by people making derogatory comments about them online.

For example, you've got Joey who is constantly being bombarded on Facebook, Twitter, and the rest about his appearance. Maybe he wears glasses, maybe he can't afford the newest style of clothes, whatever. With cyber bullying even more so than with traditional bullying, what we see happening next is people just piling onto Joey. One person makes a comment, then another, and soon we see a snowball effect where Joey now has what seems like his entire school commenting about his family being too poor to afford clothes for him.

From a child's perspective, this feels like the entire world is against them. Joey may have some support, but the positive voices are almost always quieter than the negative ones. Psychologically this is devastating for a child. A victim of bullying can experience negative effects like depression, physical illness, changes in personality, and even death. We've all heard stories about victims of bullying who were so traumatized by the constant barrage of negativity that they took their own life.

Signs of Cyber Bullying

Now that we've explored what bullying is and how it can affect kids, let's talk a little bit about signs parents should look for in order to catch bullying before it's too late. Watching for the signs of bullying can, admittedly, be difficult. Some of the main behaviors that surface while someone is being bullied include becoming withdrawn, wanting to stop going to school altogether, not hanging out with their normal group of friends, or pulling back from typical activities and actions.

The tricky thing is that all of these behaviors could be a sign of a teenager going through any one of many life stages. It becomes nearly impossible for a parent to just look at their child and think, "Hmmm, I think they're being bullied". A parent isn't a mind reader; they can't know what is actually happening in their child's life without being a part of their life. So while being mindful of the general signs of bullying is important, the only way to truly know if your child is being bullied is by talking to them.

Steps to Protect Against Cyber Bullying

This leads me into what is by far the most effective tool in protection against bullying, and that is consistent, continual, and open communication lines with your children, with their siblings, even with their friends. The idea is to be as tuned into your children's lives as possible, because it's the only way you're going to know for sure if they're having bullying issues. You have to be proactive.

Being proactive doesn't mean that I'm advocating for total control over your children's lives. Of course they need to have freedom, but as a parent it's your job to be an active participant in their life. For example, if your son or daughter wants to be on Facebook then make it a requirement that you're an unrestricted friend of theirs so you can see what is being posted on their account. Set rules about how they get to use social media, don't just sit back and assume they're responsible and mature enough to navigate issues that could arise.

Also, if your children are going to have a cell phone, tablet, or other device be upfront with them and let them know what your expectations are. When my wife and I gave our son his first cell phone we said, "Look, we're paying for this. You get to use it, but we get to monitor it whenever we want". We told him that that if he has an issue he can come to us, whether it's downloading some stupid app by accident or someone sends him an inappropriate or bullying text. We made sure he knew that if he came to us, with anything, he wouldn't be in trouble. If we found something and he didn't come to us, that's when there would be a problem.

It all goes back to open and honest communication. You don't have to be on your kids' devices every day, but monitor them once in a while and talk to them often about it. Be firm but fair and you'll be able to avoid confrontation while doing your job as a parent and protecting your family. Interact with your children, show them you're involved, follow them on Twitter, learn about Snapchat...the bottom line is that the best way to protect your children against bullying is to keep those lines of communication open.

What to Do If You Find Your Child is Being Cyber Bullied

If you find yourself in the unfortunate but common situation of having a child who is being bullied it's important to know what steps should be taken. First, reassure your child that you're going to take action, and really mean it. I've seen it happen many times where a parent tells their child they're going to take action and then they fall short. These are usually the parents who immediately give a laundry list of action steps, "I'm going to talk to your teacher, I'm going to talk to your principal, I need to contact the other kid's parents, I'm going to do X, I'm going to do Y, I'm going to do Z...". The reality is that so early on you have no idea how things will play out. Letting yourself become stressed, angry, and irrational doesn't help to deal with the situation, and in fact can make it worse. Instead, stay calm and tell your child, "Hey, I'm going to help you. I'm going to take action". Then you can make a real plan and go at it without being overly emotional and potentially adding to the problem.

The next thing to do is capture the information as quickly as possible. I call this step the Cyber Bully Information Capture System. This is a methodical system you go through where you capture and save anything that's come into your child's cell phone, computer, etc. Capture and save that information - whatever accounts, wherever possible. This is crucial because some information posted publicly may be able to be deleted by the bully, leaving you without proof. Once you have the information captured and saved, add time and date stamps wherever possible and make a presentation of everything you have. This information will be very important if you have to provide documentation for a principal, lawyer, police investigation, etc. You want to create a timeline, with an origination point if possible, in order to have as much information as possible if things escalate. It's much better to have and not need than to need and not have.

Finally, get rid of everything you can from your child's devices. You have the information saved, the next step is to try and distance your child from the effects of the bullying as soon as possible. Capture, save, and erase the information. If it's bad or threatening messages or texts, block the number of the person(s) sending the messages. If it's emails, block those emails; same with Facebook accounts and other social media. Whatever form the bullying has been coming from, however the bully is sending their information, block it to keep it away.

Also, understand that there are no guarantees that your child will be spared after the blocks take effect. People can find ways around your defenses if they're determined - setting up new profiles, recruiting others to join the bullying, etc. They might attack again, and you'll have to be diligent and block again. You should also try to stay up to date on the security features your child's devices have built into them. Look at the "readme" files on the Mac and PC platforms; they'll give you information about blocking things and restricting websites. Or just Google "top ten best security software programs for..." and fill in the blank with whatever you're trying to defend against. Ultimately, you may also have to think about making the decision of changing your child's information like their email account and phone number. If that happens, I'll go back again to reminding you to be open and honest with your child - keep those lines of communication open throughout the process.

Summary

The world is constantly changing, and cyber bullying is something that we as parents never really had to deal with growing up. It's important that we remain aware of the problem now, and that we let our children know they can come to us with any issues. The absolute most important thing is sitting down with your kids, talking with them, and making sure that they know you love and support them unconditionally. That is always going to be number one. I know that I might sound like a broken record at this point, but truly that will get you more results than anything else - making sure your kids know they can trust you and that you will take action if something happens. From there, really be willing and prepared to take whatever action is needed by having a plan for what to do before, during, and after your child comes to you with bullying concerns. We may not be able to stop bullying altogether, but we can and should be doing everything in our power to protect our children so they can stay happy and healthy.

Brett Lechtenberg is Utah's Leading Expert on Personal Safety. His martial arts school, Personal Mastery Martial Arts, is focused on developing individuals through leadership, communications skills, confidence building, family protection, and much more.

Brett is the best-selling author of The Anti Bully Program, The Anti-Cyber Bully Program, and Protecting Your Castle.

Brett continues his Personal Mastery Mission through his work with business owners and entrepreneurs to master their businesses and lives.

For more information visit www.brettlechtenberg.com

YOUR NEXT STEP: THE BUTTERFLY EFFECT

Thank you for reading this book, the latest in a series that is designed to raise awareness of the problem of the effects of bullying in our society.

While the contributing authors each have a very unique, and quite possibly, conflicting, opinion on the mechanics of becoming bullyproof, one thing is universal among all of the experts and leaders: it is up to us, as individuals in our communities to do something about it.

In your town, city or community there are numerous efforts to affect change to better the lives of kids in schools who are affected by bullying. There are organizations that will, for little or no cost, educate and advocate for kids to empower them to become their own heroes.

At this point you have a choice. You can put this book down, having collected the opinions of the best minds in bullying prevention, and you can say "Wow, that was terrific!" and go about your life as usual. And the natural consequence of this action will be that everything that has continued to be, will be.

Or, the other option is to do something. Do something in your community to make a difference. Whether it is to go to your local martial arts school and sign up your kid, or to attend a seminar with Tony Robbins to empower yourself, or even to create a support group that pledges to actively work to empower the people in your town. And the natural consequence of *this* action will be that something will be different.

You have probably heard of "The Butterfly Effect." It is the theory that small changes in a system can alter outcomes significantly. For example, the flapping of the wings of a butterfly on one side of the ocean (a seemingly insignificant action) can result in a drastic change in the trajectory of a hurricane.

What is your "butterfly effect" going to be?

How many heroes will be unleashed because of you?

It's up to you.

GETTING INVOLVED WITH THE BULLYPROOF PROJECT

The *Bullyproof: Unleash the Hero Inside Your Kid* book series is designed to raise awareness. However, awareness isn't enough. To effect true, lasting change in our communities, it requires action.

The contributing authors of the *Bullyproof* series are committed to bettering their hometowns through community involvement. Many are on speaking tours, school visits, or hold bullyproof classes. They are known as the Bully Experts in their town, the go-to source of real transformation in people.

The truth is that one can't read a book, or take one workshop, or attend one pep rally and become bullyproof. It takes time, effort, energy and commitment.

These contributing authors have missions in their businesses to help kids and adults become empowered, and the best way for them is to establish an ongoing working relationship with their clients and communities.

If you, like them, are completely committed to transforming your community and making it bullyproof, and you would like to be involved in a future volume of the *Bullyproof: Unleash the Hero Inside Your Kid* series, then we should talk.

Contact Alex at www.alexchangho.com or via email at alex@alexchangho.com and let's make a difference in our communities *together*.

Made in the USA
Monee, IL
08 July 2023